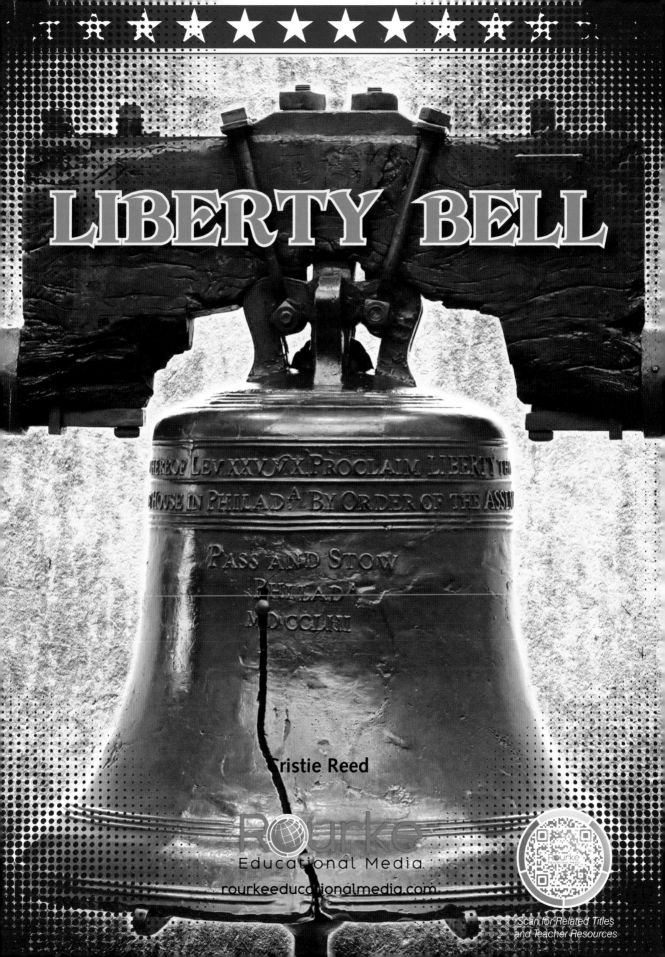

LIBERTY BELL

Cristie Reed

Rourke
Educational Media

rourkeeducationalmedia.com

Before Reading:

Building Academic Vocabulary and Background Knowledge

Before reading a book, it is important to tap into what your child or students already know about the topic. This will help them develop their vocabulary, increase their reading comprehension, and make connections across the curriculum.

1. *Look at the cover of the book. What will this book be about?*
2. *What do you already know about the topic?*
3. *Let's study the Table of Contents. What will you learn about in the book's chapters?*
4. *What would you like to learn about this topic? Do you think you might learn about it from this book? Why or why not?*
5. *Use a reading journal to write about your knowledge of this topic. Record what you already know about the topic and what you hope to learn about the topic.*
6. *Read the book.*
7. *In your reading journal, record what you learned about the topic and your response to the book.*
8. *After reading the book complete the activities below.*

Content Area Vocabulary
Read the list. What do these words mean?

abolitionist
colony
commemorate
cupola
democracy
epitomized
equality
expositions
foundation
pacifism
ratification
replica
symbolized
tolled

After Reading:

Comprehension and Extension Activity

After reading the book, work on the following questions with your child or students in order to check their level of reading comprehension and content mastery.

1. *Why was the Liberty Bell hidden during the Revolutionary War? (Summarize)*
2. *What are some of the characteristics of the Liberty Bell? (Summarize)*
3. *In what ways was William Penn a forward thinker? (Asking questions)*
4. *How does the Liberty Bell symbolize the abolitionist movement? (Infer)*
5. *What is the meaning of pacifism? (Summarize)*

Extension Activity

The Liberty Bell has been a symbol of freedom for many groups through history, including abolitionists and suffragists. What would the Liberty Bell represent today? Create a poster using the Liberty Bell as a symbol of freedom for a cause that is going on today.

TABLE OF CONTENTS

A VISION FOR LIBERTY

What's so important about a bell that's over 260 years old, cracked, and doesn't even ring? It can be traced back to a forward-thinking man named William Penn. William Penn had a vision for peace, freedom, and **equality** for all people. His vision gave power to the people and allowed them to work together to shape their own government.

Penn's vision became the **foundation** of **democracy** in the United States of America. A bell was created to **commemorate** Penn's visionary work. That old, cracked bell that doesn't ring is the Liberty Bell. It has become an international symbol of peace, freedom, and liberty for all.

WILLIAM PENN'S STORY

William Penn was born in England in 1644. Young William saw people treated unfairly in his country. He saw people punished for having different religious beliefs and for trying to speak freely. William was a serious student. He learned different ways of thinking. He decided to pursue a life in which all people were treated equally and had the freedom to make their own choices.

William Penn (1644–1718)

As a young man, William decided to become a Quaker. Quakers were a Christian group committed to **pacifism**. He worked with other Quakers to establish a settlement in America where everyone was granted freedoms not permissible in England.

William wanted everyone to be able to choose his or her own religion. He wanted people to have a voice in their government and make their own laws. No matter what religion or what race, he thought all people should be treated equally.

William Penn arriving in Philadelphia, 1682

On March 4, 1681, King Charles II granted William Penn a vast tract of land west of New Jersey. Just west of the Delaware River, Penn formed the **colony** of Pennsylvania in 1682. William Penn would govern this new colony.

Freedom Fact!

William's father, Sir William Penn, was a supporter of King George I. His son, King George II ordered the colony to be named Pennsylvania in honor of his friend Sir William Penn. Sylvania comes from the Latin word meaning "forest lands."

William Penn made friends with the Native Americans who lived in Pennsylvania. He treated them with dignity and respect and wanted other people in the New World to do the same.

Most important to Penn was the government of his colony. He planned his colony and chose land for the capital city, Philadelphia. Penn wanted to create something that had never been done before.

Penn chose the name for his capital city. Philadelphia comes from the Latin words *philos* and *adelphi*. *Philos* means "love" and *adelphi* means "brother." Philadelphia is nicknamed the City of Brotherly Love.

William Penn met with the Delaware Indians in 1771 to trade and establish a peaceful relationship.

Penn designed a frame of government for his colony. The framework included his beliefs in freedom and equality. This framework became an experiment in democracy. Penn's experiment was a success. His framework would be used as the foundation for the U.S. Constitution.

Penn and other colonists faced money problems, disagreements, and the leadership in England. Penn worked hard to govern Pennsylvania. He wanted to unite all of the colonies. In 1701, he worked with the other colonists to draw up a plan for government. Penn's famous plan became known as the Charter of Privileges.

Freedom Fact!

William Penn never saw the Liberty Bell. He died in England in 1718. His ideas for democracy remain alive in our country and in other parts of the world. The bell stands today as a symbol of his vision.

THE BELL

Fifty years after Penn's famous charter, members of Pennsylvania's state government chose to commemorate his important work. They ordered a bell to be made with the following words inscribed on it: "Proclaim Liberty thro' all the land unto all inhabitants thereof." This biblical quote **epitomized** Penn's vision for freedom.

The bell was ordered from Whitechapel Foundry in England. It arrived in Philadelphia on September 1, 1752. In March of 1753, the bell was hung in the newly built Independence Hall. But, the first time the clapper struck the bell, it cracked. Two craftsmen, John Pass and John Stow, were asked to melt down the original bell and recast a new one. Pass and Stow cast the bell and added a bit more copper to make it stronger. When the bell was tested again, many people were unhappy with the tone.

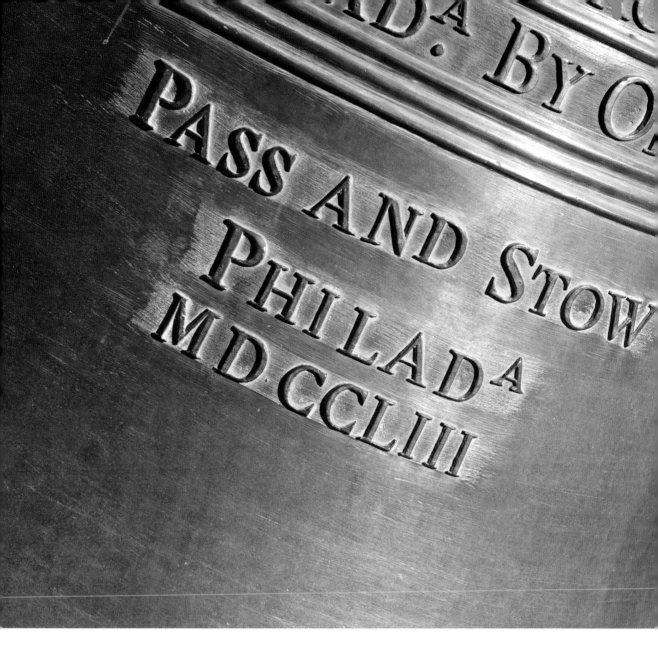

PASS AND STOW
PHILADA
MDCCLIII

Another bell was ordered to be made from the Whitechapel Foundry. When it arrived, most people thought that it sounded no better than the Pass and Stow bell. The Pass and Stow bell remained in the steeple on top of Independence Hall, also called the State House. The second Whitechapel bell was hung in the State House **cupola**, where it chimed the time for Philadelphia's citizens.

The bell was named the State House bell. Over the years, it rang to call attention to important events, call people together, and commemorate special days. The bell **tolled** to announce Benjamin Franklin's trip to England, where he addressed the colonies' grievances with the King.

The State House, 1776

Benjamin Franklin's return to Philadelphia, 1785

King George III (1738–1820)

Declaration of Independence

Stamp Act

It tolled to celebrate King George III becoming King of England. In 1764, it tolled to announce the repeal of the Sugar Act, and in 1765 to announce a meeting to discuss the British Stamp Act. Historic accounts say that the bell tolled to celebrate the first reading of the Declaration of Independence on July 8, 1776.

During the Revolutionary War, British soldiers occupied Philadelphia. Many valuables had to be hidden from the British. Across the colonies, church bells were hidden to prevent soldiers from melting them down to make cannons. The State House bell was hidden under the floorboards of the Zion Reformed Church in Allentown, Pennsylvania.

British soldiers entered cities like Philadelphia and Boston in an attempt to stop the colonists from revolting.

The bell was brought back to Philadelphia in 1778. In 1785, the old steeple where the bell hung in Independence Hall was torn down and rebuilt. The bell was hung in the rebuilt Independence Hall steeple. The bell tolled once again for the **ratification** of United States Constitution in 1787.

Freedom Fact!

The Declaration of Independence and the United States Constitution were both signed inside Independence Hall.

The characteristic that distinguishes the Liberty Bell from other bells is its famous crack. Specific details about where and when the large crack first appeared are unclear. Records show that a crack was visible when the bell rang for Revolutionary War hero, Marquis de Lafayette, in 1824. That crack expanded when the bell rang for the funeral of Justice John Marshall on July 8, 1835. Philadelphia's mayor ordered the bell to be rung in recognition of George Washington's birthday in 1846. After that occasion, the crack expanded further and the bell could no longer ring.

Cracks occurred frequently in bells made during this time period. The metals used to make them became brittle. Drilling can prevent cracks from spreading. The crack on the State House bell had expanded too far and drilling could not prevent further cracking.

The Bell's first note

LIBERTY BELL FACTS

Owner	City of Philadelphia
Original Strike Note	E-flat
Composition	70 percent copper, 25 percent tin, 5 percent other metals
Yoke Wood	American Elm

Original Weight	2,080 pounds (943 kilograms)
Weight of Yoke	200 pounds (90 kilograms)
Circumference at Lip	12 feet (3.66 meters)
Thickness at Lip	3 inches (7.62 centimeters)
Circumference at Crown	7.5 feet (2.29 meters)
Thickness at Crown	1.75 inches (4.45 centimeters)
Height from Lip to Crown	3 feet (0.91 meters)
Height Above Crown	2.25 feet (0.68 meters)
Length of Clapper	3.16 feet (0.96 meters)
Weight of Clapper	44.5 pounds (20 kilograms)
Length of Drilled Crack	24.5 inches (62 centimeters)
Width of Crack	0.5 inches (1.3 centimeters)
Length of Hairline Crack	28 inches (71 centimeters)

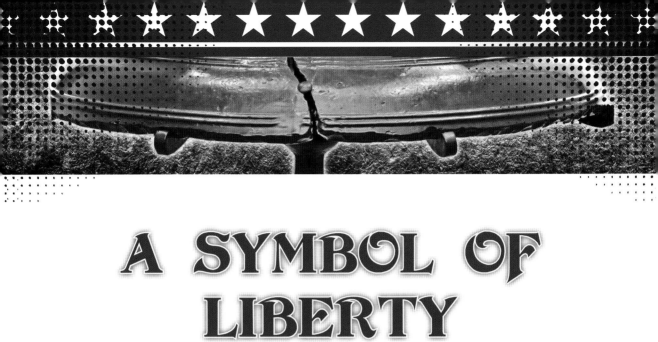

A SYMBOL OF LIBERTY

In the 1830s, groups of people wanted to put an end to slavery, racial discrimination, and segregation. Many of these people were part of the **abolitionist** movement. They adopted the bell as their symbol because of its inscription.

William Penn's ideals fit with abolitionists' beliefs in freedom and liberty for all. In 1837, an image of the bell appeared on an antislavery publication. The bell **symbolized** a country that was divided. The crack symbolized the way that freedom was broken for its African American citizens.

The abolitionists began calling the bell, the Liberty Bell. That name appeared over and over in antislavery publications. The name caught on with everyone.

The Liberty Bell *was an antislavery publication that featured verse, editorials, and songs by writers and celebrities of the day.*

After the Civil War, the Liberty Bell became a symbol of unity for the United States. The Liberty Bell was used to help heal the country after the long war.

From 1885 until 1915, the Liberty Bell traveled around the country. It was displayed at world's fairs and international **expositions**. The United States wanted to show its best images to the world. Wherever the bell went, crowds came out to get a glimpse of this great American symbol.

In 1915, women did not have the right to vote. To help promote equality for women, a **replica** of the Liberty Bell, the Justice Bell, traveled through Pennsylvania, Chicago, and Washington, D.C. The bell's clapper was chained to its side to keep the bell silent, which symbolized women's lack of a voice in government.

The image of the silent bell was used to support women's desires for the same rights as men. Women finally received the right to vote in 1920. In September of that year, the Justice Bell was returned to Independence Hall in Philadelphia. The clapper was unchained and the bell rang to celebrate their victory.

Freedom Fact!
Women's right to vote was ratified by the Nineteenth Amendment to the U.S. Constitution on August 18, 1920.

I VOTED!

That old, cracked bell truly became the people's bell. The Liberty Bell represents the hopes and dreams of many Americans.

TIMELINE

1751 —— *Pennsylvania's General Assembly commissions the Liberty Bell to commemorate the fiftieth anniversary of Penn's Charter of Privileges.*

1752 —— *In September, the bell arrives in Philadelphia from the Whitechapel Foundry in England.*

1753 —— *In March, the bell is hung in the State House steeple in Philadelphia. It was rung and cracked by the stroke of one clapper.*

1753 —— *In April, the bell is melted down and recast by John Pass and John Stow. It was hung in the State House steeple.*

1754 —— *In March, a third bell is ordered from Whitechapel Foundry in England. It was used in a cupola for the State House clock.*

1776 —— *The bell rang for the first public reading of the Declaration of Independence on July 8.*

1777 —— *The bell is taken down and hidden in the floorboards of the Zion Reformed Church.*

1837 —— *The bell appears on the front of an antislavery publication and is given the name "Liberty Bell."*

1846 —— *The Liberty Bell tolls to commemorate George Washington's birthday. Its crack expands.*

1852 —— *The Liberty Bell is brought down from the steeple and placed inside Independence Hall.*

1915 —— *The Liberty Bell travels across the country to the Panama-Pacific Exposition in San Francisco, California.*

1976 —— *The Liberty Bell is moved from Independence Hall to a bicentennial facility on Independence Mall.*

2003 —— *The Liberty Bell is moved to its current location at the Liberty Bell Center in Philadelphia.*

Liberty Bell Center

GLOSSARY

abolitionist (ab-uh-LISH-uh-nist): someone who worked to abolish slavery before the Civil War

colony (KOL-uh-nee): a territory that has been settled by people from another country and is controlled by that country

commemorate (kuh-MEM-uh-rate): something done to honor and remember an important person or event

cupola (KOO-puh-luh): a small dome on a roof

democracy (di-MOK-ruh-see): a way of governing a country in which the people choose their leaders in elections

epitomized (e-PIT-o-mized): a highly accurate example

equality (i-KWOL-uh-tee): the same rights for everyone

expositions (ek-SPOH-zi-shuhns): large exhibitions

foundation (foun-DAY-shun): the basis of something

pacifism (PASS-i-fism): the belief that war and violence are wrong

ratification (rat-i-fuh-KAY-shun): a formal approval

replica (REP-luh-cuh): an exact copy of something

symbolized (SIM-buh-lized): stood for or represented something else

tolled (TOHLD): rang slowly and regularly

INDEX

SHOW WHAT YOU KNOW

1. Explain how the Liberty Bell became a symbol of freedom and equality for so many people.
2. What reasons does the author give to support the claim that William Penn was a founder of democracy in the United States of America?
3. Explain the sequence of events related to the creation and hanging of the Liberty Bell.
4. Compare how the Liberty Bell was used in the late 1700s and early 1800s to how it was used in the late 1800s and early 1900s.
5. How do William Penn's forward-thinking ideas connect to the symbolic meaning of the Liberty Bell?

WEBSITES TO VISIT

www.ushistory.org/libertybell

www.nps.gov/inde/liberty-bell-center.htm

www.majesticrecord.com/libertybell.htm

ABOUT THE AUTHOR

Cristie Reed is a long-time teacher of reading. She currently lives in Florida with her husband and pet dog, Rocky. She loves to travel. Traveling in the United States of America has taught her to appreciate our great country. She hopes all kids enjoy studying the history of the United States of America and the people who worked to make it great.

Meet The Author!
www.meetREMauthors.com

www.rourkeeducationalmedia.com

PHOTO CREDITS: Cover © Racheal Grazias, Petrov Stanislav; page 5 © David Sucsy; page 6, 7, 8, 9, 14, 18, 23 © Wikipedia; page 10, 14, 15, 17, 24, 25, 26 © Library of Congress; page 13 © Shane Morrison Photography; page 15 © seregam; page 16, 22 © North Wind Picture Archives; page 19 © Rebekah McBride; page 20 © Edwin Verin; page 26 © Steve Debenport; page 27 © Pamela Albin Moore; page 29 © aimintang

Edited by: Jill Sherman

Cover design by: Nicola Stratford, nicolastratford.com
Interior design by: Rhea Magaro

Library of Congress PCN Data

Liberty Bell / Cristie Reed
 (Symbols of Freedom)
  ISBN 978-1-62717-738-2 (hard cover)
  ISBN 978-1-62717-860-0 (soft cover)
  ISBN 978-1-62717-971-3 (e-Book)
Library of Congress Control Number: 2014935663

Printed in the United States of America, North Mankato, Minnesota

Also Available as: